Leader's Guide

Guided Meditations for Advent, Christmas, New Year, and Epiphany

A QUIET PLACE APART

Leader's Guide ❄❄❄❄❄❄❄❄❄❄❄❄❄❄❄

Guided Meditations for Advent, Christmas, New Year, and Epiphany

Jane E. Ayer

Saint Mary's Press
Christian Brothers Publications
Winona, Minnesota

Genuine recycled paper with 10% post-consumer waste.
Printed with soy-based ink.

The publishing team included Robert P. Stamschror, development editor; Jacqueline M. Captain, copy editor; Alan S. Hanson, production editor and typesetter; Maurine R. Twait, art director; Elaine Kohner, illustrator; cover photo copyright © Chad Ehlers, International Stock photo; pre-press, printing, and binding by the graphics division of Saint Mary's Press.

The acknowledgments continue on page 48.

Printed in the United States of America

Printing: 9 8 7 6 5 4 3 2 1

Year: 2005 04 03 02 01 00 99 98 97

ISBN 0-88489-517-3

Contents ❄❄❄❄❄❄❄❄❄❄❄❄❄❄❄

To Aggie . . .

whose favorite season is Advent and

whose sterling love, shared faith, and generous support

have been an advent of much joy and many blessings

in my life

Directions for Leading the Meditations

LEADER PREPARATION As the meditation leader, your preparation is especially important to the success of a guided meditation. Pray the meditation before leading a group in it. This will help you to become comfortable with its style and content. Some material may require a brief doctrinal review with the group. By praying the meditation first, you will become aware if there is a need to do this.

If you choose to have your group do the optional art expression as a follow-up to the meditations, it is best if you try it out before the group gathers to make sure it works well and to know better what directions to give.

If you intend to guide the meditations yourself rather than use the accompanying cassette or compact disc, rehearse the guided prayer, including the introductory comments, the scriptural reading, and the opening and closing prayers, so that appropriate and sufficient time is allowed for the imagery to take place and for prayerful reflection to occur. The meditations should be read slowly and prayerfully, using soft instrumental music as a background.

Only a good reader who has prepared should read aloud the scriptural passage that precedes each guided meditation. The scriptural passage is important to establishing the theme and the tone of the meditation. Read it with reverence and expression, using a Bible.

PARTICIPANT PREPARATION To introduce praying a guided meditation, it might be helpful to explain that the participants will be using a prayer form that will call upon their imagination, and that the Holy Spirit graces our imagination during prayer to help us to communicate with God. Remember that this type of prayer may not be easy for everyone in the group. Some may be self-conscious about closing their eyes; some may have difficulty getting in touch with their feelings; some may have personal obstacles in their relationship with God. Be gentle, let go, and let the Spirit work. In fact, participants can be told that although the meditation is guided, if the Spirit leads them in another direction, it is okay for them to go with their own reflection and not worry about the words being spoken.

A possible difficulty, one that may not be apparent at first, may be encountered by those who wear the type of contact lenses that prevent them from closing their eyes for an extended period of time. Invite these participants to put their head down, hiding their eyes in the dark crook of their arm, if they are unable to remove the lenses. Another possible difficulty may be experienced by those who have a sinus problem or asthma. Instead of breathing through their nose during the deep-breathing exercises, they can breathe quietly through their mouth.

MUSIC Quiet instrumental music is important for setting and keeping the mood of the meditation. Music can be playing even as the group gathers. It is a nice background for giving instructions. Have additional tapes or compact discs ready to play during the activities after the guided meditation. Ideally, the follow-up activities will take place in a separate space; therefore, it is less disruptive if cassette or CD players are already set up in the different areas.

REFLECTION QUESTIONS Allowing time for the participants to reflect and name the experience they have just gone through is a necessary part of these prayer experiences. The reflection questions will help the participants do this successfully. Choose several reflection questions (or use questions similar to them) and type them up, leaving room after each for a response. Make a copy for each participant. Allow enough time for each person to respond to the questions and to share his or her responses with the group. These prayer experiences are not meant to be rushed.

To avoid disrupting the quiet mood of the meditation time, pass out the reflection questions (placed facedown) as the participants take their places. Also give a pen or pencil to each person. If people are sitting on the floor, you could give out hardcover books or clipboards to facilitate writing. Explain that you are distributing reflection questions for use after the meditation.

Assure the participants that their responses are private and that their papers are not going to be collected. When it is time for sharing, honor and affirm all responses, and respect those persons who do not wish to answer aloud.

ART EXPRESSION AND PRAYER RITUAL (OPTIONAL)

Each prayer experience comes with an optional art expression containing a prayer ritual. You might choose to use this rather than the reflection questions.

If you choose to do the optional art expression, prepare the art materials ahead of time and lay them out in the area where the participants will work. Familiarize the group with the art activity before the prayer time, if possible, so as not to disrupt the meditation mood. This should allow you to give particular directions for the art activity without having to answer a lot of questions. If you have previously completed the art expression, it might be helpful to show your sample artwork at this time.

SETTING

It is imperative that the area for the prayer experience is quiet—no ringing of telephones, bells, and the like. If necessary, put a sign on the outside of your door: Praying! Please do not disturb!

Participants may sit in chairs or find a comfortable position on the floor, but they must be a few feet from one another so that they each have their own space and do not distract one another. Therefore, the area must be large enough so the participants are not cramped. Lying down on the floor should be discouraged, as some participants are likely to fall asleep.

CENTERPIECE (OPTIONAL)

Each theme of the prayer experiences can be enhanced by creating a centerpiece that can be placed on a small table, an altar, or the middle of the floor. The centerpiece should include objects that reflect the message of the prayer, a Bible opened to the scriptural passage, and candles. For example, for the meditation on Advent ("Naming"), you might make a centerpiece with an advent wreath, and statues or pictures of Mary and Elizabeth and the angel Gabriel. The participants' first names could be written on slips of paper and placed around the centerpiece.

A centerpiece for the meditation on Christmas ("Birthing") should include a nativity scene complete with shepherds and Magi. It might also display a small, lit Christmas tree.

For the meditation on New Year's ("Offering"), you might burn a small amount of incense, if no one is allergic to it. The smoke wafting upward is symbolic of our prayer and offerings going "upward" to God. A box, crate, low stool, or cloth-covered table can serve as the altar of offering or sacrifice. Place an ornate tray on the altar as well, and surround your centerpiece with lit candles.

To enhance the meditation on Epiphany ("Journeying"), the centerpiece should include the nativity scene, or at the very least, the Magi and camels and a figure of baby Jesus laying on hay. Knapsacks and gift boxes or beautiful tins could also be used.

MATERIALS NEEDED FOR EACH MEDITATION

- a Bible
- an audiotape or CD player
- the meditation recording or script
- tapes or CDs of instrumental music
- reflection questions (a copy for each participant)
- pens or pencils
- clipboards or hardcover books to facilitate writing, if needed
- materials for the art expression (optional; see individual project's needs)
- a centerpiece to reflect the theme (optional)
- a sign that reads Praying! Please do not disturb!

> On one hand, there was no shelter, extreme fatigue, labor pains, humble surroundings, simple shepherds, and bleating sheep; and then, on the other hand, there were singing angels, a glorious star, three Magi, a new baby, proud parents, and exquisite joy. We can come to experience peace in the midst of our personal chaos by reconciling pain and joy in the hush of our quiet place.

OPENING Read aloud this opening prayer:

> Wonder-Counselor, Prince of Peace, King of Glory, we celebrate your birth! We ask you now to guide us in our own birthings and in the acceptance of pain and joy in the areas of our life that need your presence to touch us with your peace, joy, and light. Help us to reflect in our quiet place apart with you on those things, people, or situations that require us to risk and give birth, so that our life may be like that of the angels, glorifying you always. We ask this through your holiest of names. Amen.

SCRIPTURE Read aloud Luke 2:1–20, using a Bible.

SCRIPT Play the "Birthing" meditation on the accompanying recording or slowly and reverently read aloud the following script for the guided meditation. Play soft, instrumental background music.

> Today you will enter the hush of your quiet place and meet Jesus in your imagination. First, you will begin by doing some deep-breathing exercises. When I say to, if you can, breathe in and out through your nose very quietly during these exercises. Close your eyes and get comfortable. You will be relaxing your entire body.
>
> Breathe in deeply . . . hold it . . . breathe out slowly and completely. Breathe in deeply . . . hold it . . . breathe out slowly and completely.

Again, breathe in deeply . . . hold it . . . breathe out slowly and completely.

Allow your feet and ankles to relax. Relax your legs . . . and your hips. . . . Stay mindful of your breathing. Relax your stomach muscles . . . and now your chest. . . . Just relax. . . . Let your arms grow limp. . . . Relax your wrists, . . . your hands, . . . and your fingers. . . . Keep breathing in deeply and out slowly and completely.

Allow your shoulders to become heavy. . . . Let all the tension drain from your shoulders. . . . Relax your neck, . . . your facial muscles, . . . and even your eyelids. . . . Just relax. . . . Breathe in deeply . . . hold it . . . breathe out slowly and completely. [Pause.]

You are in a room with a Christmas tree, a candle in the window, and a beautiful manger scene. The tree and candle are lit, and there is a soft glow to the room. It is a peaceful space. Go over and look closely at the manger scene. Think about the people whose lives are represented there. They had a hard life. Pick up each figurine as you reflect on them: Mary, who became a pregnant teenager and gave birth in a manger with no mother or father there to share in her joy, who suffered immensely to witness her son's persecution; Joseph, who married Mary rather than shame her, who bore the responsibility to find a birthing place for his wife, who felt the crunch of financial strain in his poor surroundings; Jesus, who was born as an innocent babe, who was to grow up and accept the humiliation of rejection, who was to suffer the anguish and torment of a cruel death; the shepherds, who slept on hillsides with their sheep rather than on soft beds, who were surrounded by smell and noise constantly, who were simple folk and poor; the Magi, who traveled blindly, achingly sore on camels, who were astronomers desperately wanting to find purpose to their journey.

You now think about what is hard in your life. [Pause.]

Look at the figures in the manger scene again. These same people had moments of joy in their lives. Mary gave birth to a healthy Son who was God, the Word made flesh. She had a devoted Joseph who cared for and protected her. As a mother, she filled with pride at the gentleness and compassion that her Son showed to others. She possessed a deeply religious Jewish faith. She was to come to be honored by all, blessed among women.

Joseph delighted in his Son and his wife. He taught Jesus his skill at carpentry. He loved and obeyed Yahweh to whom his heart was always open. Jesus was nurtured by two loving parents. He grew into the realization of his oneness with God. He turned his healing love, peace, and mercy toward others, and so, he rose triumphantly.

The lowly shepherds were chosen to be heralded by angels of the birth of the Messiah. They were chosen to be invited to enter the manger and rejoice, their lowly position elevated by this honor. The Magi did not fail in their efforts for they found the King and presented him their gifts of gold, frankincense, and myrrh; and, they played a part in history by safeguarding Jesus from Herod.

You now think about what is good in your life and what have been moments of joy in your life. [Pause.]

There is a sound at the door. You look over to find Jesus standing there. Hear him greet you by name and wish you his peace. . . . Invite him to sit with you. . . . Listen as Jesus tells you that giving birth . . . all the times when you allow for newnesses or change or growth in your life . . . is both painful and joyful. . . . Jesus tells you that he understands that is what your life has been like. . . . He tells you that has been the experience of his family, his friends, and his own life, too. . . .

Jesus invites you to share with him the areas of birthing that you need to consider. . . . Hear him ask you what newnesses, growth, or change you might be avoiding because of the pain involved. . . . Is something scary for you? Take this time to talk for a while together about the areas of growth you want to succeed at and the things that are in your heart that possibly keep you from facing new births in your life. [Pause.]

Now talk for a moment about what the benefits will be to risk birthing in these areas. . . . You name what joy you might feel because of newness, change, or growth. Share openly with Jesus. [Pause.]

Promise Jesus that you will open yourself up to give birth to what is in the womb of your heart. . . . Listen as Jesus lovingly tells you that he has great confidence in you. . . . Hear him as he assures you that he will be with you always in both the pains and the joys of your birthings. . . . He tells you that your life will be to him like the angels', glorifying him forever. . . .

It is time for Jesus to go now. His warm and gentle hands touch you in blessing. . . . Listen quietly to the prayer that he says just for you. . . . It is very moving and you will remember it always.

> . . . Say your good-byes in whatever way is special to you. . . . Walk Jesus to the door. Return and sit again in the peace and the soft glow of the room, remembering this time of new birth for you. . . .
>
> Breathe in deeply . . . hold it . . . breathe out slowly and completely. Breathe in deeply . . . hold it . . . breathe out slowly and completely. Once more, breathe in deeply . . . hold it . . . breathe out slowly and completely. And when you are ready, you may open your eyes.

REFLECTION Continue to play instrumental music. Ask the participants to reflect on the experience that they have just gone through by pondering some of the following questions. You might want to suggest that they respond to those questions that speak most to them. Allow time for them to write their reflections.

- How did it feel to sit quietly in the room with the Christmas tree, the light in the window, and the manger scene?
- What was it like to examine the hardships of the lives of the people in the stable? Did anyone's hardships strike me in particular?
- What is hard in my life right now?
- What was my reaction when I examined the joys in the lives of the people in the manger scene? Did anyone's joys strike me in particular?
- Describe what is good about my life. What moments of joy do I remember?
- How did it feel to have Jesus come and visit?
- What birthings—newness, change, or growth—did I share with Jesus that I need to focus on?
- Am I afraid of anything? If so, what? Did Jesus help me with my fears?
- What benefits will come with risking and giving birth? Can I hold on to them?
- Can I allow myself to feel the confidence that Jesus has in me? Why or why not?

- Do I trust that Jesus will be with me in my pains and joys? Why or why not?
- Can I believe that my life will be like the angels', glorifying Jesus?
- What emotion was I experiencing when Jesus blessed me and said a prayer for me?
- What were our good-byes like?
- What is the most special message or image that I am taking away with me from this prayer experience?

ART EXPRESSION AND PRAYER RITUAL (OPTIONAL)

The art expression is an optional activity. It can be used in place of the reflection questions. If you decide to use this activity, prepare the art area before the group gathers. At a place for each participant, have pencils, crayons or markers, and a sheet of art paper.

After the meditation, continue playing quiet music in the art area. Invite the participants to move to one of the prepared places. Direct them to draw, symbolize, or name—in the center of their art paper—the nativity figure whose life touched them the most during the reflection. Around that, instruct them to use colors or symbols to represent their own personal hardships and joys, and the birthings they hope to risk and experience.

Explain that sharing faith experiences can help to strengthen one another's faith. Then invite the participants to take turns sharing the figure that moved them, and the symbolism and the colors they used. Add that when they finish sharing their individual art expression, they are to place their artwork in the center of their prayer space near the manger scene. Invite them to pray, "Prince of Peace, I am open to birthing" or something similar as they set their art down.

Allow enough time for the sharing and affirming of each person. Continue playing instrumental music, as it helps with reverencing the moment. Encourage the participants to place their art expression in a visible place in their own homes—perhaps near their nativity scene—as a reminder of their time with Jesus and their openness to new birth. Remind the group that they can return to their imagination at any time and be with Jesus in this very real way.

For closure to the meditation experience, read aloud the following prayer:

CLOSING

Wonder-Counselor, King of Glory, Prince of Peace, we thank you for this time of quiet prayer and your visit to us. We are grateful for the new awareness of the lives of those who were at the manger. Help us now to be as strong as they were as we face areas of new birth, change, or growth in our life. Give us the compassion and acceptance needed to help others as they face their birthings.

Please grace us with a sense of reconciliation between the pains and joys of our life so that we do not become bitter or empty. Fill us now with your courage and lasting peace, so that our life may always be like that of the angels, glorifying you forever. Amen.

New Year Offering

This soul-searching prayer experience is based on the Presentation in the Temple when Mary and Joseph, in the Jewish tradition, brought baby Jesus to be presented to the Most High. Here they also offered a sacrifice to God. It reminds us that we, too, must make our offerings and give sacrifices that will be pleasing to the Lord.

THEME After you have given directions to the participants and set the tone for meditation, introduce the theme by saying something like the following:

> It is important for us to spend time in reflection so that we can identify the goals and sacrifices we wish to make in this New Year. We need to examine where we are in our life areas and renew our commitment to that which

> we have lovingly promised in the past. It is time to present our offerings; we can discover them and lift them up in the hush of our quiet place apart.

OPENING Read aloud this opening prayer:

> Mary and Joseph, you stood proudly in the Temple with your most precious offering and your sacrifices. Because of your deep and holy relationship with your God, you knew what would be pleasing to the Most High. Help us to spend this time in quiet, so that we can be open to the same Spirit who touched your hearts, so that we can do some sincere soul-searching and present to the Most High the offerings of our goals and sacrifices for the New Year, and so that the living out of our days may bring us peace and give God praise and glory. We ask this through the intercession of you both. Amen.

SCRIPTURE Read aloud Luke 2:21–40, using a Bible.

SCRIPT Play the "Offering" meditation on the accompanying recording or slowly and reverently read aloud the following script for the guided meditation. Play soft, instrumental background music.

> Today you will enter the hush of your quiet place and meet Mary and Joseph in your imagination. First, you will begin by doing some deep-breathing exercises. When I say to, if you can, breathe in and out through your nose very quietly during these exercises. Close your eyes and get comfortable. You will be relaxing your entire body.
>
> Breathe in deeply . . . hold it . . . breathe out slowly and completely. Breathe in deeply . . . hold it . . . breathe out slowly and completely. Again, breathe in deeply . . . hold it . . . breathe out slowly and completely.

Allow your feet . . . and ankles to relax. . . . Relax your legs and your hips. . . . Keep in touch with your breathing. Relax your stomach muscles . . . and now your chest. . . . Just relax. Let your arms grow limp. . . . Relax your wrists, . . . your hands, . . . and your fingers. . . . Keep breathing in deeply and out slowly and completely.

Allow your shoulders to become heavy. . . . Let all the tension drain from your shoulders. . . . Relax your neck, . . . your facial muscles, . . . and even your eyelids. . . . Just relax. . . . Breathe in deeply . . . hold it . . . breathe out slowly and completely. [Pause.]

You are in Jerusalem in the outside court of the Temple. . . . It is noisy, as a crowd of people swarm about you in the courtyard. Many are bringing gifts God has given them . . . gifts that represent all the blessings they have received from God. . . . It is their desire to return gifts to God in thanksgiving for God's goodness. Some bring animals . . . others bring fruits. It is the best of what they have. More people are coming into the courtyard. . . . You see a beautiful young Jewish woman enter, holding a little-more-than-a-month-old baby. . . . With the mother and child is a quiet and serene Jewish man carrying a cage with two turtledoves and an ornately carved wooden tray under his arm. . . . He has his other hand beneath the young woman's elbow to steady her through the crowd. . . . You know them. . . . They are Mary and Joseph with their infant Son, Jesus! . . . Joseph gets in line to leave his turtledoves with one of the Temple priests. . . . The birds are the young couple's gifts that represent the offering of their child back to the most high God—the most high God who has given them this precious boy child. In doing so they redeem their firstborn Son according to the Law of Moses.

Joseph returns to Mary and the baby, and as a family they start toward the Temple stairs. . . . Mary says something to Joseph and nods in your direction. Then Joseph walks over to you with a warm smile on his face. . . . Hear him say your name and tell you that he and Mary would like you to be part of the ceremony of the Presentation of their Son in the Temple. . . . Notice what you are feeling to be invited. . . .

Quietly you walk together up the steps and open the two huge Temple doors made of cedar. . . . You step into the first room called the porch. It is a hallway that allows the loud bustle of the courtyard to be left behind as you go further into the Temple. . . . You notice it getting quieter. . . . Each of you stop and remove your shoes. . . . You will be entering a holy place. Reverently you begin the long walk into the main part of the Temple. Mary and Joseph bow thirteen different times as they approach the inner sanctuary. Prayerfully you do what they do. [Pause.]

In the main chamber now, allow yourself to see its magnificence—the pillars and archways, the tapestry that covers the altar up at the far end, and the gold and silver overlay. . . . High windows let in the afternoon sunshine which illumines everything. . . . Smell the incense as it burns sweetly from two small side altars. . . .

Join Joseph and Mary as they walk closer to the altar. . . . By the look on their faces, you sense it is special for them to be here in this sacred space.

Joseph is getting ready for something. Watch as he quietly positions the beautifully carved tray between both his strong hands. You sense that Joseph has carved it for this moment . . . for his Son. . . . Mary lovingly lays Jesus upon the tray and kisses his tiny face. . . . Joseph looks proudly and happily at his Son. . . . Joseph approaches the steps of the altar and passes his most precious and valuable offering to the *kohen,* who is the Temple's priest.

This religious man loudly asks Joseph if he wishes to redeem his Son or to leave him here with the *kohen.* . . . Hear Joseph reply clearly that he desires to keep his Son. . . . The *kohen* raises the baby high three times and announces each time, "Your Son is redeemed. . . ." Observe the joy, yet, humbleness in Joseph's and Mary's faces as their Son is lifted high. . . . It is apparent that this offering of their Son back to the Lord is from their heart.

Simeon and Anna, two very old and faith-filled people, approach Mary and Joseph. Simeon takes Jesus into his arms and praises God. . . . You watch as his gnarled hand gently strokes the baby's face. . . . His entire being begins to shake with tremendous excitement. He announces clearly that he can die peacefully for God has fulfilled the promise of salvation. . . .

Simeon touches Joseph and Mary in blessing. . . . Listen as he tells Mary that her Son will suffer in bringing salvation to God's people . . . and that she, too, will feel a sword pierce her heart. . . . You see Joseph put his arm around Mary, protectively. . . .

Anna now reaches for the baby. . . . Tears of gladness course down her wrinkled face as she lifts up her trembling voice in thanksgiving to God. Mary and Joseph bend their heads silently as Anna prays. . . .

Move a little off to the side by yourself. Take this time to reflect slowly and honestly on your goals, anticipations, and resolutions for the New Year. Allow this self-examination to help you do some soul-searching. Allow this time to help you discover the best of who you are . . . in the image and likeness of the God who gifted you with every good thing. This is the you to be returned as offering to the Most High. Perhaps there will be some effort needed on your part to become an offering more pleasing to the Lord. Know that these efforts of yours will be the gifts that will represent you as an invaluable offering to the most high God. Just listen quietly as different life areas are presented to you for later reflection.

What personal goals for the New Year do you need to focus on in your life areas? What choices do you need to make to remove stress from your life? What relationships do you need to cultivate into healthier ones? What habits, character flaws, or attitudes do you hope to improve, so that your life reflects you as God intended you to be? Do you anticipate hurt or suffering that might be yours in the New Year? Can you offer it up like Mary and Jesus? Is there anything that you can decide to give up or let go of to become more whole and peaceful? Quietly reflect on these. You will be discovering and naming your New Year's resolutions and the beautiful offering of yourself that you can present to the Most High. [Pause.]

Mary and Joseph leave the baby with Anna and Simeon and walk closer to you. It is time. They gently guide you to the altar so that you can raise up to the Most High your resolutions and the offering of yourself. It is the best God has given you; the gift of yourself. It is the best you can return. Lift your arms high. You notice Mary and Joseph also lifting their arms in prayer with you as you present what is in your heart to the Lord, your God. Speak your full offering out loud. [Pause.]

Hear Mary say your name and tell you that the grace of God is upon you. . . . Hear Joseph wish you courage in the effort that you will be putting into this New Year. . . . Notice what you are feeling as Mary and Joseph extend their hands in blessing over you, and you listen to their prayer filled with caring words. [Pause.]

It is time for the Holy Family to go now. Anna and Simeon return the baby to Mary. Say good-bye to each of them in whatever way is comfortable for you. . . . Watch as they quietly leave the Temple to lead a life that will ultimately be given for you. . . . Remain here for a moment and relive what has just happened. . . . Recall your treasured offering to the Most High—the gift of who you are. [Pause.]

Breathe in deeply . . . hold it . . . breathe out slowly and completely. Breathe in deeply . . . hold it . . . breathe out slowly and completely. Once more, breathe in deeply . . . hold it . . . breathe out slowly and completely. And when you are ready, you may open your eyes.

REFLECTION Continue to play instrumental music. Ask the participants to reflect on the experience that they have just gone through by pondering some of the following questions. You might want to suggest that they respond to those questions that speak most to them. Allow time for them to write their reflections.

- What was it like for me to be in a crowd at the outer courts of the Temple and see people bringing their offerings for God to the Temple priests?
- Did I feel anything in particular when I noticed that the new couple and baby coming into the yard were Joseph, Mary, and Jesus?
- What did I notice feeling when Joseph approached me and invited me into the Temple for his son's ceremony?
- Was I moved or affected by the reverent way we entered the Temple, such as the removal of our shoes and the thirteen times we bowed?
- What was my image of the Temple? What impressed me the most?
- When Mary laid Jesus on the tray and Joseph approached the altar and *kohen,* what was I thinking or feeling?
- What was my impression of the ceremony? Was I struck by any part of it? If so, what touched me?
- How do I think Mary and Joseph felt when Simeon and Anna approached and said what they did? Have I ever felt what they were possibly feeling? If so, when?
- In order to discover more clearly the gift that I am, on what will my efforts be focused for the New Year in regard to the life areas below?
    - spirituality and prayer
    - health
    - family, friends, community, or parish
    - education
    - work or career
    - recreation and relaxation
    - choices to take the stress out of my life
    - relationships: unhealthy ones, new ones, former ones
    - habits, character flaws, or attitudes
    - services
    - sacrifices

- So that my life reflects me as God intended me to be, how might I improve my habits, character flaws, and attitudes?
- What service might I perform to give selflessly to God's Reign?
- Do I anticipate any hurt or suffering this New Year? If so, what is it? Can I offer it up like Mary and Jesus?
- Is there anything that I can decide to give up or let go of to become more whole and peaceful?
- What was it like to go up to the altar with Mary and Joseph on each side of me and present myself aloud as an offering to the Most High? What did I say?
- Could I feel the grace of God upon me when Mary told me that it was? Will I allow Joseph's wish of courage to help me in my efforts during the New Year?
- What were Mary and Joseph's caring words of blessing as they extended their hands over me? What were my emotions or thoughts during this?
- In what way did we express our good-byes to each other?
- Am I renewed with a sincere sense of commitment to my New Year? Why or why not?
- What is the most special message or image that I will remember from this prayer experience?

ART EXPRESSION AND PRAYER RITUAL (OPTIONAL)

The art expression is an optional activity. It can be used in place of the reflection questions. If you decide to use one of these activities, prepare the art area before the group gathers.

After the guided meditation, continue playing quiet instrumental music in the art area. Invite the group to move quietly to one of the prepared places.

Art Expression 1

At each place have a sheet of art paper, crayons or markers, and pencils. Direct the participants to draw their most memorable scene within the Temple in the middle of the art paper. This can be done abstractly by using just splashes or designs of color to depict the feelings and thoughts they experienced by being at Jesus' Presentation in the Temple with Mary and Joseph or by their discovering, lifting up, and naming the New Year's offering at the altar. Some individuals might want to draw the scene itself in a more realistic fashion which is fine. Instruct them to use colors that speak about how they were feeling or what they were thinking. Around the completed scene, invite the participants to use other colors or symbols to denote what their offerings for the New Year will be.

Art Expression 2 At each place have a bookmark-size (2" x 6" or larger) piece of white art paper, crayons or markers, different colored yarn, and clear contact paper (if you do not have a laminating machine). Have several paper punches and scissors available.

Instruct the participants to choose a word or words to write on their bookmark that will be a reminder of their offering. Have them use color as a way of expressing the feelings that they experienced during this prayer time . . . and how they feel about the New Year ahead. They are free to decorate their bookmark in any way that is meaningful for them.

Direct the participants to cover their bookmark on both sides by enclosing it in clear contact paper and cutting off the excess. Using the paper punch, have each put a hole in the top about a quarter of an inch down. Next, have them choose a piece of colored yarn to thread through the hole. Have them knot the ends together and leave as a fringe.

After either art expression, explain that sharing faith experiences can help strengthen one another's faith. Then invite the participants to share their prayer experiences by explaining the colors, words, or symbols on their artwork that they feel comfortable naming. Add the instruction that as each individual completes his or her sharing, the artwork is to be placed on the offering tray or altar in the prayer center. Invite them to overlap their artwork with one another's as a sign that they will pray for one another in the living out of the New Year. Suggest that as they approach the center, they might lift their artwork up high (with or without the tray), and then place it down while praying, "Accept my offering, O Most High God . . ." or something similar.

Allow enough time for the sharing and affirming of each person. Continue playing instrumental music, as it helps with reverencing the moment. Remind the participants that they can return to their imagination at any time and be with Mary and Joseph in this very real way. Encourage them to place their art expression in their home in a visible spot to remind them of their New Year's offerings.

CLOSING For closure to the meditation experience, have different participants lead the following prayer of petition:

Response
May the grace of God be upon us this New Year.

Leader
In our offerings to be more faithful to our spirituality and prayer life . . . [All respond.]

Leader
In our desire to take better care of our mental, emotional, and physical health . . . [All respond.]

Leader
Within our plans to be more present to our families, friends, communities, or parishes . . . [All respond.]

Leader
In our choices regarding education, our work, or our career . . . [All respond.]

Leader
During our times of recreation and relaxation . . . [All respond.]

Leader
As we make difficult choices to remove or minimize stress in our life . . . [All respond.]

Leader
In our efforts to develop or preserve relationships that are valuable and healthy . . . [All respond.]

Leader
During our sincere endeavors to correct or control our bad habits, character flaws, or attitudes . . . [All respond.]

Leader
Within our decisions to be of service to and make sacrifices for the Reign of God . . . [All respond.]

[Additional petitions may be added at this time.]

Most High God, accept our offerings to you as we strive to please you and to bring you greater glory. Grant us the grace and courage that Mary and Joseph assured us would be ours to face this New Year. Allow our soul-searching to make us more aware of what we must change, accept, or do in order to be faithful to you as were Mary, Joseph, Jesus, Simeon, and Anna despite the pain or hardships encountered.

Finally, make us a selfless people whose service to and sacrifices for others will promote justice and peace for all. We lift this prayer and our offerings up to you. Amen.

Epiphany Journeying

This challenging prayer experience is based on the scriptural passage of the three Magi who traveled blindly, except for the light of an uncharted star, to find and present their gifts to the Messiah. It invites us to look deeply within ourselves, to discover the gifts we have been given, and to be open as to where we must journey in order to bring to the manger the finest of our treasures.

THEME After you have given directions to the participants and set the tone for meditation, introduce the theme by saying something like the following:

> It is a special honor to be able to come before our King and present unique gifts as did the Magi with their personal presence and their gold, frankincense, and myrrh. To do the same, we need to quiet ourselves and

> look within so that we can discover lasting gifts to give and the journey we must make in order to give them. We will be able to uncover what they might be and where we need to go in our life if we willingly enter our quiet place apart.

OPENING Read aloud this opening prayer:

> King of Glory, allow us to feel your gift of peace, so that we can escape any noise or busyness that would keep us from discovering where we might find you and what we can offer you. We pray that even our effort to reflect quietly right now is a sign of our desire to journey closer to you like the Magi did. May your presence be experienced as we open up our heart to learn where you would have us travel and what you would have us give, so that we will bring you praise and glory as the Messiah. We ask this now King of Glory, Prince of Peace. Amen.

SCRIPTURE Read aloud Matthew 2:1–12, using a Bible.

SCRIPT Play the "Journeying" meditation on the accompanying recording or slowly and reverently read aloud the following script for the guided meditation. Play soft, instrumental background music:

> Today you will enter the hush of your quiet place and meet Jesus, Mary, and Joseph in your imagination. First, you will begin by doing some deep-breathing exercises. When I say to, if you can, breathe in and out through your nose very quietly during these exercises. Close your eyes and get comfortable. You will be relaxing your entire body.
>
> Breathe in deeply . . . hold it . . . breathe out slowly and completely. Breathe in deeply . . . hold it . . . breathe out slowly and completely. Again, breathe in deeply . . . hold it . . . breathe out slowly and completely.

Allow your feet and ankles to relax. Relax your legs . . . and your hips. Keep in touch with your breathing. Relax your stomach muscles, and now your chest. . . . Just relax. Let your arms grow limp. Relax your wrists, . . . your hands, . . . and your fingers. . . . Keep breathing in deeply and out slowly and completely.

Allow your shoulders to become heavy. . . . Let all the tension drain from your shoulders. . . . Relax your neck, . . . your facial muscles, . . . and even your eyelids. . . . Just relax. . . . Breathe in deeply . . . hold it . . . breathe out slowly and completely. [Pause.]

It is nighttime. You are traveling safely by yourself over hills and through fields. . . . You carry a walking stick and a knapsack on your back. . . . A bright star in the sky gives you hope and direction. You keep walking. . . . You hear sheep bleating over to your right, but you do not see them. . . .

Somewhere a shepherd plays on a flute and the quiet music fills the air. . . . As you walk, you think about where you must travel in your life to become closer to the Christ. . . . You think about what decisions you need to make, . . . what relationships need your attention, . . . what gifts you possess that you have not developed fully or used faithfully, . . . what you might need to give up or get rid of in your life to become more whole. . . . Find a place to sit down so that you can reflect deeply on these areas. . . . Let the peacefulness of the night air surround you and provide safety in which to think. [Pause.]

Pull your knapsack over onto your lap. . . . Inside of it are gifts from the King, the Prince of

Peace, to you. Open your knapsack and begin to discover what the Lord of Light has given you to help you fully celebrate your life. . . . Spend some time with the gifts that you have received. They are what you will need to continue your life's journey. Allow yourself to understand the meaning they have for you. [Pause.]

Stand up now. It is time to complete this journey. . . . As you continue to follow the starlight, you notice that it begins to be growing brighter as you start to climb the next hill. . . . Look up into the night sky and watch the star for a moment. . . . What is it that you feel? . . . Stop at the top of the hill and look down toward a cave nestled in the foot of the next hill. . . . Shapes of animals seem to be quietly roaming about. . . . People are highlighted by a lantern hung in the manger. . . .

This place seems to possess its own warmth and light. It is very welcoming. You walk toward this warmth and light. . . . You are met by Mary and Joseph, and shepherds and kings who come out to greet you. . . . They express their gladness that you have come. . . .

Now they separate and step back so that you can see the babe who is swaddled in a white blanket and cushioned by sweet-smelling hay. . . . The baby reaches toward you. . . . Notice what you are feeling. . . . Slowly and reverently kneel and allow yourself to be one with the joy and wonder that emanates from the manger. . . . Open your knapsack and remove the gifts that were given to you. . . . Place them at the foot of Jesus as an offering. . . . You are returning to him your most treasured possessions. Allow it to be your pledge that you will use his gifts as your gifts as you continue life's journey. [Pause.]

Hear Mary say, "My Son is well pleased with your gifts. . . ." Joseph nods in agreement. Listen as he says, "Thank you. You have given him the gold from your heart. . . ." You don't have to leave just yet; so spend some time just absorbing the goodness and holiness that surrounds you. Allow it to be the source of strength that you need to travel through your days and nights ahead in all your life areas. Take a last look at the gifts that you and the King of Glory have exchanged together. Your remembrance and use of them will be a sign of his presence and your desire to always bring him praise and glory.

It is time to leave now. Say your good-byes to everyone in a way that is comfortable for you. Begin walking up the hill. Look back as many times as you need to the warm light emanating from the manger. . . . Know that you are taking with you—on your life's journey—the memory of this night and the gifts you have been given.

Breathe in deeply . . . hold it . . . breathe out slowly and completely. Breathe in deeply . . . hold it . . . breathe out slowly and completely. Once more, breathe in deeply . . . hold it . . . breathe out slowly and completely. And when you are ready, you may open your eyes.

REFLECTION Continue to play instrumental music. Ask the participants to reflect on the experience that they have just gone through by pondering some of the following questions. You might want to suggest that they respond to those questions that speak most to them. Allow time for them to write their reflections.

- How did I feel to be walking in the fields and over hills on a starlit night by myself?
- Could I imagine the sheep bleating and the flute being played?
- When I stopped and reflected, where did I think I must travel in my life to become closer to Christ?
- What decisions do I need to make? Did this prayer experience help me with them?
- What are the gifts that I have not developed fully or used faithfully?
- What is it that I might need to give up or get rid of in order to become more whole?
- Name the gifts that were in my knapsack from the King, the Prince of Peace.
- Was I surprised to have received them? Was I surprised by any of them in particular?
- Describe the meaning each gift has for me.
- What did I feel when I looked down the hill and saw the manger for the first time?
- Explain the emotion that was mine when I was greeted by Mary, Joseph, the shepherds, and the Magi, and when I saw Jesus for the first time.
- Did I feel something special when Jesus reached for me? If so, what was it?
- Was it hard for me to leave my gifts at the manger? Why or why not?
- Will I remember these gifts and allow them to sustain me in my life?
- How did I feel when Mary and Joseph complimented me?
- What is the most special message or image that I am taking with me from this prayer experience?

ART EXPRESSION AND PRAYER RITUAL (OPTIONAL)

The art expression is an optional activity. It can be used in place of the reflection questions. If you decide to use one of these activities, prepare the art area before the group gathers.

After the meditation, continue playing quiet music in the art area. Invite the group to move quietly to one of the prepared places.

Art Expression 1 Set a place for each participant with a dinner-size, all-white paper plate, and crayons or markers. Instruct the group to express with color or symbols the gifts that were in their knapsacks. Tell them that the roundness of the paper plate reflects their desire for wholeness. Remind them that the King, the Prince of Peace, has given them gifts to bring them toward wholeness.

Art Expression 2 Set a place for each participant with a gift box of any size, bows, ribbons, slips of paper, markers or crayons, and pens. Instruct the participants to write on their slips of paper the gifts that were found in their knapsack. Encourage them to color or draw on their box and decorate it to reflect how they feel.

After either art expression, explain that sharing faith experiences can help strengthen one another's faith. Then invite the participants to share their artwork and the symbolism within it. Invite them to name the gifts that they found in their knapsacks. Add the instruction that when each individual is finished sharing that she or he is to place the artwork in the center of the prayer space, around the manger, or any other designated place. They might want to pray, "King of Glory, thank you for my gifts; I return them to you with love" or something similar as this is done.

Allow enough time for the sharing and affirming of each person. Invite each participant to place their art expression around their manger at home or in some special place as a reminder of this prayer time and as a sign of their returning their gifts to the King, the Prince of Peace, by using them in daily life. Remind the participants that at any time they can return to the manger in their imagination and spend time with the Holy Family.

CLOSING For closure to the meditation experience, have different participants lead the following litany of thanksgiving.

Litany Response
Prince of Peace, King of Glory, we thank you.

Leader
For the brilliant Christmas star and the example of the Magi's courage . . . [All respond.]

Leader
For the journey that you call us on to become closer to you . . . [All respond.]

Leader
For the gifts that you have given us on the way . . . [All respond.]

Leader
For this special time of reflection with you . . . [All respond.]

Leader
For the strength to make decisions in our life that will be pleasing to you . . . [All respond.]

Leader
For the courage to give up or get rid of that which is not good . . . [All respond.]

Leader
For the persons in our life who have been like gold to us . . . [All respond.]

Leader
For the treasure of your love . . . [All respond.]

Invite the participants to add their own prayers of thanksgiving.

ACKNOWLEDGMENTS
(continued)

To Fr. Robert Stamschror, my editor and a "real" person, I am truly grateful for his expertise, humor, and regard—each of which fosters for me such an enjoyable work relationship . . . and to the publishing team for their hard work and professionalism, much gratitude!

Deep appreciation to Barry Russo, whose extraordinarily moving instrumental music nourishes the meditations into more prayerful experiences for all those who engage in them.

To Rabbi William Kaufman, PhD, of Temple Beth El in Fall River, Massachusetts for his warm welcome into his synagogue and community and for his aid in researching the background of the "Offering" meditation in this publication, I am most especially grateful.

Kudos to Anthony "Barrel" Marrapese of Reel to Real Recording Studio, Cranston, Rhode Island, for yet another fine production championed by his patience and laughter.

To Aggie, Isabel, Shirley, Eileen, Jean, Cheryl, Alycia, Pete, Sr. Mary George, Pauline, Fr. Jude, Aunt Mary, Sue, Marie, Laura, Marlene, Claire, Soupie, Pat, Kathy, Lisa, the Doyles, Libby, Belle, retreat and workshop participants, and family members, especially my children and grandchild—I embrace you and thank you.

Other titles in the Quiet Place Apart series available from Saint Mary's Press

Each of the titles in this series by Jane E. Ayer (formerly Arsenault) has a leader's guide and recordings of the meditation scripts. The leader's guide contains directions for preparing the meditations, the meditation scripts, and suggestions for follow-up after the meditations. The audiocassette and the compact disc contain high-quality recordings of the meditation scripts along with a background of original music.

Guided Meditations for Junior High:
Good Judgments, Gifts, Obedience, Inner Blindness

Leader's guide: 0-88489-500-9, 7½ x 9¼, 48 pages, stitched, $9.95
Audiocassette: 0-88489-501-7, 90 minutes, $8.95
Compact disc: 0-88489-502-5, 90 minutes, $14.95

Guided Meditations for Adults:
Salvation, Joy, Faith, Healing

Leader's guide: 0-88489-393-6, 7½ x 9¼, 48 pages, stitched, $9.95
Audiocassette: 0-88489-394-4, 90 minutes, $8.95
Compact disc: 0-88489-424-X, 90 minutes, $14.95

Guided Meditations for Youth on Personal Themes

These guided meditations are on the themes of new life, discipleship, self-esteem, and secrets.

Leader's guide: 0-88489-347-2, 7½ x 9¼, 46 pages, stitched, $8.95
Audiocassette: 0-88489-354-5, 90 minutes, $7.95

Guided Meditations for Youth on Sacramental Life

Jane E. Arsenault and Jean R. Cedor

These guided meditations are on the four sacraments of baptism, confirmation, the Eucharist, and reconciliation.

Leader's guide: 0-88489-308-1, 7½ x 9¼, 40 pages, stitched, $8.95
Audiocassette: 0-88489-309-X, 90 minutes, $7.95

"Jane Ayer's meditations offer a rich retreat from our hurried and often frantic lifestyle. Her work gently and peacefully leads to the quiet place within all of us where God dwells and is present to those who search." **Deacon Bruce Bonner,** diocesan director of religious education, Diocese of Fall River, Massachusetts

"In my four years as a high school chaplain, I have consistently used guided meditations with our youth. In any given weekly session, at least forty to sixty students, often more, voluntarily attend. I am a firm supporter of guided meditations and have seen the positive effects they have on spiritually thirsty, and sometimes, spiritually starving, teenagers." **Fr. Kevin Fisette,** Bishop Hendricken High School, Warwick, Rhode Island